MW01259750

THE FIRST BOOK OF

MACHINES

By WALTER BUEHR

Pictures by the Author

© 2017 Living Library Press
Bristol, Virginia, 24201

This work was originally published in 1962 by Walter Buehr,

with illustrations by the author and was published by the

Franklin Watts Company of New York.

Living Library Press has brought this book back into print because of its
creative and timeless relevance to the study of machines.

Contents

The FIRST BOOK of

MACHINES

THIS BOOK is about the story of modern machines, and how they do the world's work. We shall see how raw materials, such as metals, wool and cotton fibers, and wood, are turned into automobiles, ships, typewriters, fabrics, and other useful products. Our machine age has made this possible, for only by machines can these many products be made cheaply and quickly.

We shall also see how machines are able to do such varied jobs as threshing grain, machining engine blocks, or multiplying long rows of numbers. And later on, we shall learn how automation, the newest marvel of the machine age, teaches machines almost to "think" for themselves.

A World Without Machines

IN ORDER for us to compare the wonders of our modern machine age with the days of hand tools, let us take an imaginary trip back through medieval England. How was work done in that age?

We find ourselves following a rough pathway between green hedges that leads us to a field where peasants are preparing the soil for spring planting. One man loosens the earth with a kind of broad-bladed pick, called a *mattock*. Other men follow behind, breaking up the lumps and smoothing the ground with rakes and hoes. Then the sowers, carrying bags of seed hung around their necks, cast handfuls of seed about them as they stride across the field.

When harvest time comes, other peasants will cut the grain with hand sickles, and tie it into bundles which they will carry to the barns on their backs. In the barnyard they will beat the kernels from the stems with long, hinged sticks called *flails*, toss the straw into the air with forks for the wind to carry away, and then shovel the kernels into sacks.

When flour is needed to bake bread, the medieval housewife pours a handful of grain kernels into a hollowed-out stone slab called a *mortar*. Then she grinds them into a coarse flour with a rounded stone called a *pestle*.

As we approach a medieval sawmill, two men are sawing boards from a big log that is lying across a high framework. One man stands on top of the log holding one end of a long saw, while the other stands beneath it and pulls the other end. It is slow, hard work—it will take them many hours to saw out just one plank.

Farther on, we pass some medieval "traffic"—groups of men, women, and children carrying great loads on their backs, as well as donkeys, horses, and even dogs, straining under heavily loaded pack saddles. Sometimes a rough, two-wheeled cart passes, its solid wheels screeching on ungreased axles. It is pulled by oxen or horses at a rate of two miles an hour.

At the edge of a small market town, we pass a new house being built. The walls have timbered frames, filled in with stones or bricks; the roof is thatched, built of tight bundles of straw wedged together. The carpenters are making door and window frames, using crude saws, planes, and chisels. The windows have only wooden shutters, for there are no glass blowers as yet in England to make windowpanes.

In an open doorway a shoemaker sits at his bench, cutting cowhides into boot soles and uppers; these he will put together with needle and thread and wooden pegs. A woman sits before a clacking hand loom, patiently passing a shuttle back and forth between the *warp*, or vertical threads, and crossing them with the *woof*, or horizontal threads. It is the only way she knows to make cloth.

Loud hammering is coming from another doorway. Here a coppersmith is beating copper sheets into pots, pans and jugs. Next door a tailor sits cross-legged on his table and stitches a sleeve into an armhole.

In medieval times all work, whether in field, forest, village, or town, had to be done with crude hand tools. Handwork was slow, for human muscles soon tired. There was no way of speeding production beyond what human fingers could do.

The First Machines

NO ONE knows exactly how long ago it was that the first simple machine was invented. Perhaps it was a rough grindstone mounted on an axle and turned with a crank, or a potter's wheel, worked by a foot treadle, to turn a chunk of clay into a jar or pot. Whoever invented that first machine started a new era—an era in which men

4

would slowly but surely be relieved of the back-breaking toil of making things solely by hand.

Exactly what is a machine? A machine is any device that helps you do work faster and with more power than by using your hands alone. It does this by using any one of, or any combination of, the following six basic aids: the inclined plane, the wedge, the lever, the wheel and axle, the screw, and the pulley. These six could really be considered four, because the wedge is just another form of the inclined plane, and the screw is an inclined plane wrapped around a cylinder, or drum.

These aids are often called *simple machines.* Combinations of several simple machines are called *complex machines.* With a simple machine like a lever, a man can multiply his lifting power so many times that he can easily lift a weight that ten men couldn't lift without the lever. With a wedge he can split great logs or even rocks. With pulleys and a rope tackle he can lift great loads into the air without help—loads that a whole gang of men couldn't lift an inch with their muscles alone. In other words, a simple machine can multiply the amount of force applied to a task.

The speed of a machine can also be increased by connecting a large wheel to a smaller one by means of a belt, chain, or gears, and applying power to the large wheel. The smaller wheel will turn much faster, speeding up the action. The old-fashioned spinning wheel, the sprocket and chain of a bicycle, or the transmission of an automobile are examples.

But the speed with which such a machine does its work depends upon the *kind of power* applied to that big wheel. In the earliest machines, man power was used to turn a crank, to work a foot treadle, to haul on a rope tackle, or to push the bars of a *windlass,* a kind of drum which winds up a rope as it turns.

HAND CRANK TO POWER
EARLY WOOD LATHE   WINDLASS OVER EARLY MINE SHAFT

Because those early machines depended upon manpower, they naturally slowed down as soon as the human muscles got tired. Later, horses, cattle, and even dogs were used to turn treadmills and windlasses, but even though they had more endurance than men, they, too, were living creatures and also grew tired. This is why some other kind of power than flesh and blood had to be found if machines were ever to reach their full usefulness.

Then someone thought of harnessing the power of wind and water. Windmills and water wheels became the chief sources of power until well into the nineteenth century. They were used to pump water, saw lumber, grind grain, press oil, and turn the machines of factories.

Water and wind power were a big improvement over men and animals, but they also had their limitations. When the

6

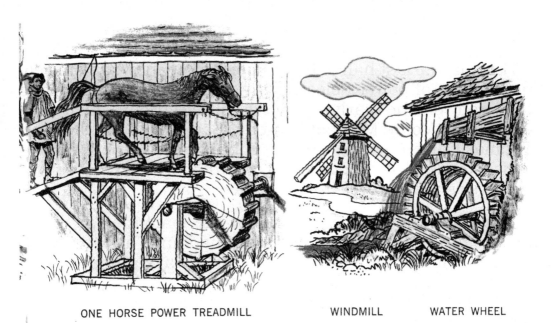

ONE HORSE POWER TREADMILL   WINDMILL   WATER WHEEL

wind died, the arms of the windmills stopped turning; so did the machinery in the mill below. If a rainless period dried up the streams, soon there was not enough water in the millpond to turn the wheel. Thus, the mill was out of business until it rained.

Then, early in the 1700's a Scottish boy named James Watt, while watching the steam rising from his mother's teakettle, thought of a new source of power. Why couldn't steam power be used to run machines? As he grew older, this idea kept him experimenting. Finally he succeeded in inventing a steam engine that could do many things. It was used to pump water from the tunnels of coal mines, turn machines in factories, and work the grindstones in flour mills. When the steam engine was mounted on wheels it would pull cars along a track—the first railroad.

With the steam engine it was possible to build factories even where there were no rivers to turn water wheels. The steam engine was always ready to go. If more power was needed, bigger engines could be built to supply it.

Then, in the last half of the nineteenth century, an entirely new source of power—electricity—came into use. Following the lead of the early pioneers of electricity—men like Alessandro Volta, Michael Faraday, Benjamin Franklin, and Thomas Edison—engineers began building electric dynamos which made electric power—power that could be sent out over wires to wherever it was needed.

Now the time was really ripe for the machine age. Men had begun to learn how to design machines able to do all sorts of things; moreover, there was always a dependable supply of steam or electric power to run them. People everywhere needed and wanted the products that machines alone could produce.

WATT'S ROTATIVE ENGINE

The Modern Machine

WHAT DO we demand of our modern machines—how ɑo ᴜᴇᴄy do their jobs? To begin in with, machines can be broadly divided into the following three classes:

1. Machines that make the machines that turn out the products everyone needs and wants.

2. The machines that make these products.

3. The machines that are themselves products, like automobiles, type-writers, and bulldozers.

Machines That Make Other Machines

At the beginning of the long process of turning raw materials unto useful products are the steel and other metal mills. *Smelting plants* melt down the iron, copper, and other ores in great furnaces to recover the metals.

To make steels of different kinds, crude iron is combined with various chemicals at high temperatures. *Rolling mills* squeeze these rough steel chunks into flat, workable shapes; then great drop hammers and presses change them into useful shapes such as sheets, wire, beams, rails, and rods. From these shapes, called *stock*, the machines in a shop turn out their products.

Large factories usually have their own *foundries,* buildings in which metal castings are made. Here chunks, or *ingots*, of iron or steel are re-melted and poured into molds made of special sand compounds where they harden into the shape of the molds. Then the molds are knocked off and a rough metal object, called a *casting*, is left. This now goes to the machine shop to be machined. Many small factories buy their castings, sheets, and rods from the foundries and rolling mills.

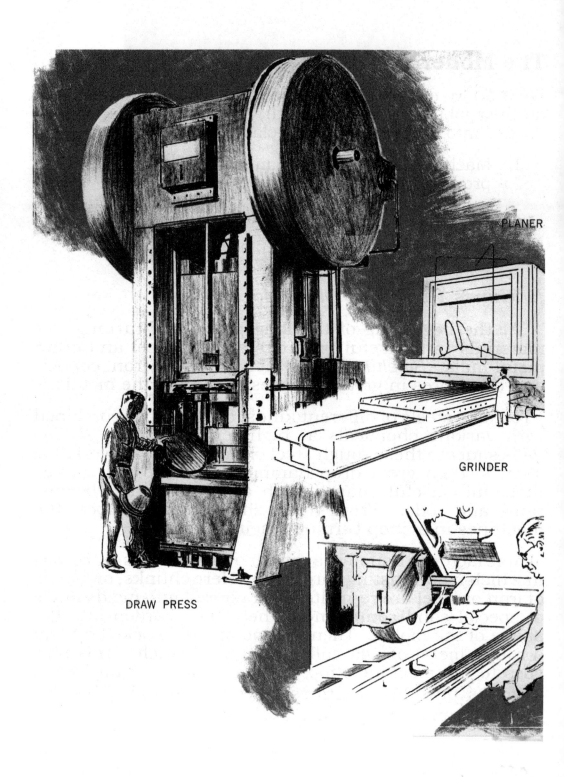

PLANER

GRINDER

DRAW PRESS

SHEARS

GEAR CUTTER

GEAR CUTTER

To make the thousands of parts which will eventually be assembled into lawn mowers, adding machines, or motor trucks, many special machines are needed. Here is a list of machines usually found in a well-equipped machine shop:

LATHES—Generally used to turn and shape rounded, or *cylindrical*, stock.

BORING MILLS—Used to finish holes where great accuracy is required.

DRILL PRESSES—To drill holes where less accuracy is re quired.

PUNCH PRESSES—To punch out shapes from flat steel (as a cookie cutter does).

SHEARS—To cut apart sheets of steel.

GRINDERS—Used to smooth surfaces and grind down edges.

PLANERS—To plane down metal surfaces to proper thickness.

MILLING MACHINES—To cut grooves and gear teeth and to bevel edges.

SCREW MACHINES—To cut spirals in blank cylinders, making screws of them.

SAWS—Band or circular, to saw through metal.

However, *only when they are properly guided and directed* can any of these machines do its job of boring holes, cutting threads and gear teeth, milling grooves, or grinding down cylinders. Unless every hole and groove on the part is cut in exactly the right place—sometimes to an exactness of one ten-thousandth of an inch—the part will be useless.

But how can the stock be held in place—sometimes at an angle—and the drill or milling cutter guided to do its task at just the right place so that each part turned out will exactly match every other one? This is done with devices called jigs, fixtures, and dies. *Jigs* and *fixtures* are specially

12

designed devices in which the part to be worked on can be held rigidly in position in the machine. Then the boring or cutting tool, held in place by a contrivance called a *chuck*, will strike the part at just the right place.

A *die* is a specially made part of very hard steel that acts as a pattern or guide. Perhaps a part has to have a shallow groove pressed into the center of a flat surface. The diemaker makes his die in two halves. He cuts out a groove in the lower half, then carves the upper half so that a ridge remains

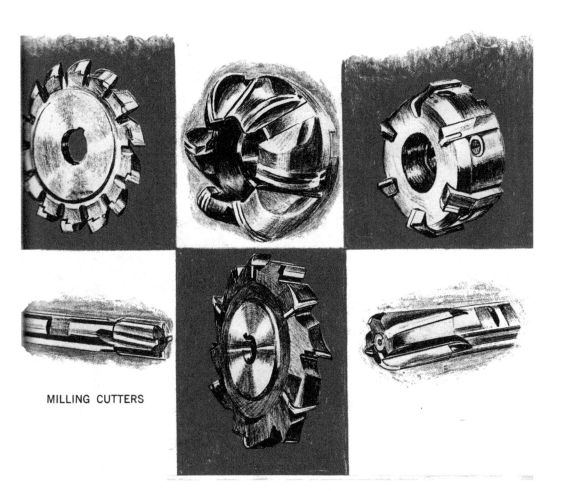

MILLING CUTTERS

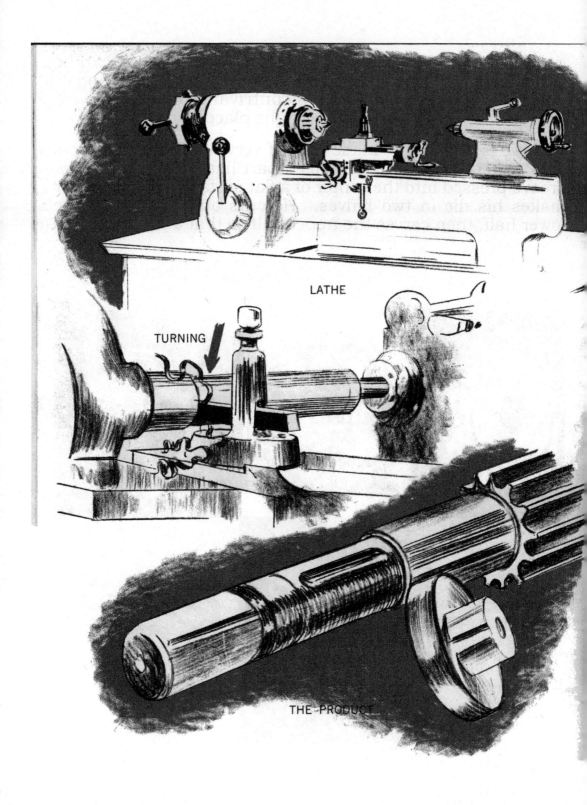

LATHE

TURNING

THE PRODUCT

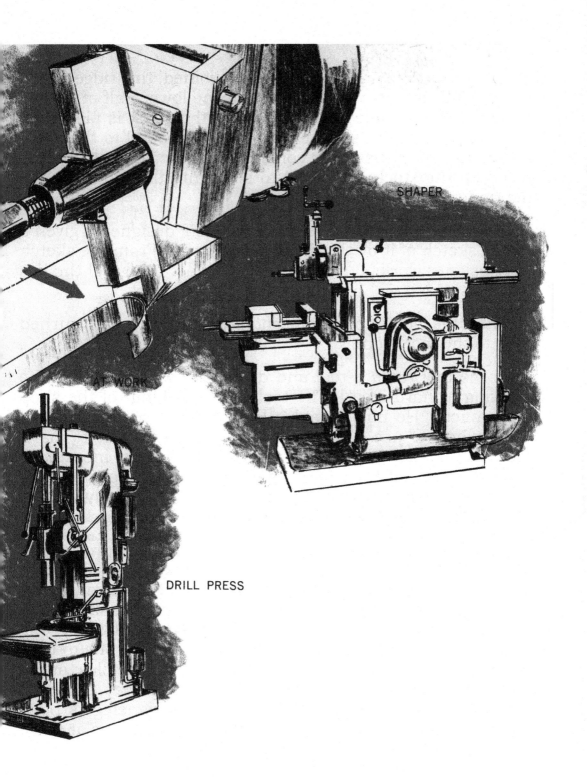

AT WORK

SHAPER

DRILL PRESS

sticking up. When the two halves are joined, this ridge will fit exactly into the groove below. Then the lower half of the die is bolted to the table of the machine, the stock is placed on top of it, and the upper part of the die is bolted to the press above it. When the press comes down, the ridge is pressed down on the stock, forcing it to bend into the groove in the die underneath.

When a new part is to be made, the tool designer is given a rough sketch of it by the department head. From the sketch the designer works out on paper the exact design of the jigs and dies which will be needed to make the part.

Then his plans, called *mechanical drawings*, are turned over to the tool room.

In the tool room a tool and die maker will reproduce the drawing in hard steel. The toolmaker is "king" of the shop mechanics. He has served a long apprenticeship to learn exactly how to use every tool, and he must be able to make dies with almost unbelievable accuracy. His measuring instruments, called *calipers* and *micrometers*, are able to measure the thickness of a piece of steel so precisely that by comparison a sheet of tissue paper would seem thick.

Machine designers are constantly trying to improve their machines so that they can turn out work better, cheaper, and faster. For example, a certain piece of work may need one hole bored through the center of it, two smaller holes drilled in at an angle, and a double groove cut along one edge. Normally this would take three machines, one to bore the center hole, a drill press to bore the smaller holes, and a milling machine to cut the groove. Doing it this way, however, makes the job slow and costly. So the designer gets busy and plans a machine that can do all three operations at once.

16

Today there are turret lathes and other machines capable of working on a part from all sides and from any angle all at once. In early machine shops it took a good deal of moving from one machine to another to make an automobile engine block. Today one single machine bores out cylinders and valve ports, drills holes for bolts, and does all the other necessary operations at one time.

How Power Is Applied to Machines

A BIG problem in designing any machine is how to apply power where and how it is needed. Power reaches the machine by way of a belt drive or an electric motor, constantly turning in one direction at the same speed. Yet one gear may have to revolve five times faster than another, or a rocker arm must move up and down *and* sideways, while a valve must open and close. How can the steadily turning motor translate its power into all these different movements? This is done by the use of cams, valves, clutches, belts, ratchets, cranks, linkages, and gears.

How a Gasoline Engine Works

Look at the drawing of a gasoline engine which has been cut away to show how the parts work. The power comes from an explosion in the cylinder head, which in turn drives the piston down in a straight line. However, a revolving motion is needed to make the automobile's wheels turn. To accomplish this, a connecting rod is suspended from a pin, called a wrist pin, in the piston, so that the rod can swing from side to side like the clapper of a bell. The bottom end of the connecting rod ends in a ring which fits around a bearing of the crankshaft. This crankshaft is held firmly in place by bearings in several places so that its cranks can revolve around the center of the shaft.

17

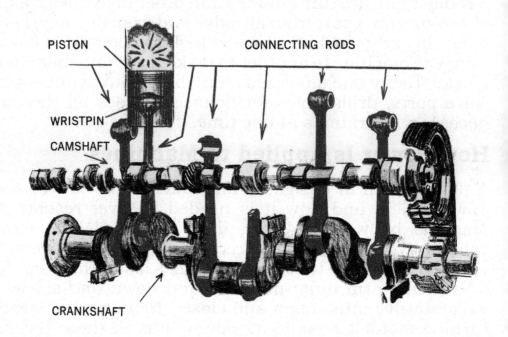

PISTON
CONNECTING RODS
WRISTPIN
CAMSHAFT
CRANKSHAFT

When the gasoline from the car's tank is mixed with air in the carburetor, it forms a vapor, which is sucked into the cylinder head and exploded by a spark from the spark plug. The explosion forces the piston down, and then the connecting rod pushes against the crank and makes it turn. When you ride a bicycle, your muscles are the "explosion," or power impulse, your legs are the connecting rods, and the pedals and sprocket are the crankshaft.

Now look at the picture of the cams and camshaft. One of the many uses of cams is to open and close the valves on a gas engine. When they are open, vapor is sucked into the cylinder. Next the valve must close tight so that the vapor can be compressed and exploded. Then

18

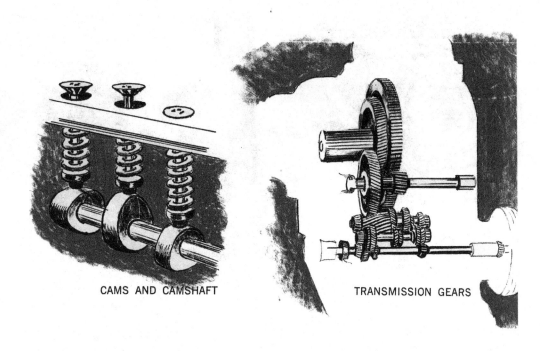

CAMS AND CAMSHAFT   TRANSMISSION GEARS

it must reopen to let out the burnt gases and be ready to suck in more fresh vapor. All this must happen with split-second timing.

The bottoms of the valve stems rest on the cams, each one held down tightly by strong springs. As the camshaft turns, the high part of the oval-shaped cam forces the valve stem up and holds it open just long enough. Then, as the cam revolves, the spring pushes the valve stem down, closing the valve.

Look at the accompanying picture of an automobile transmission. This is a good example of applying power when it is needed. A car needs a lot of power to get started or to climb a steep hill, but much less after it is moving fast

19

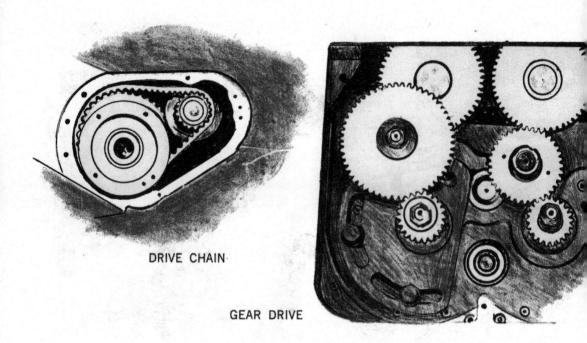

DRIVE CHAIN·

GEAR DRIVE

on a level stretch. The engine would overheat, wear out faster, and use too much gas if it always had to run as fast as when it was starting. The transmission makes it possible to turn the rear wheels faster without speeding up the engine. This is how it works.

The crankshaft of the engine is connected to one shaft that ends in a gear in the transmission. Another shaft geared to the rear axle runs forward into the transmission, and also ends in a gear. As soon as the engine starts, the gear at the rear end of its shaft turns, but the car won't move until the gear on the rear-end shaft is connected to the engine shaft. To start the car, the gearshift lever must be turned to low speed. This slides a large gear into place so that its teeth *mesh* (engage) with those of the gears on the two shafts; then the car begins to move. When second gear is engaged, it pushes a smaller gear into mesh. And when the smallest, or high, gear is

20

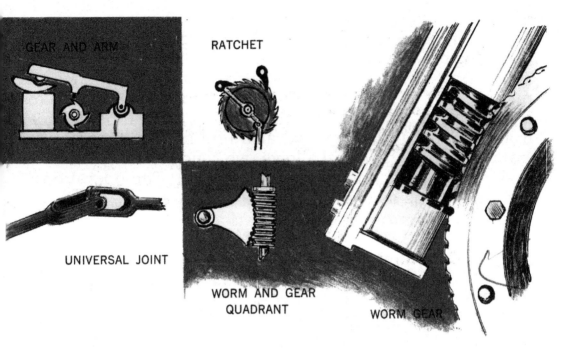

GEAR AND ARM

RATCHET

UNIVERSAL JOINT

WORM AND GEAR
QUADRANT

WORM GEAR

engaged, the drive shaft revolves even faster, although the engine is still turning at the same rate. To back the car, a reverse gear is meshed into place.

Now look at the picture of a drive chain. When for some reason the teeth of two gears cannot be made to mesh, the power may be transmitted by a chain, whose links fit over the teeth of the gears. On a bicycle the power applied to the sprocket through the pedals is carried back to the teeth of the rear-wheel axle by the bicycle chain. Because this axle is much smaller than the sprocket, the rear wheel revolves many times while your feet on the pedals turn only once.

The picture of the clockwork-gear train shows gears of many different sizes, all meshing. While the motor or spring which drives them always turns at the same speed, the gears turn at different speeds, according to their sizes.

The picture of a gear and pivoted arm shows how revolving power is changed to up-and-down motion. As the small gear turns, it forces the arm up until it reaches the highest part of the teeth; then the arm drops and makes a connection. The *pawl* in the next picture stops the gear from turning until a pivoted arm lifts it up and out of the way. The *universal joint* allows two rigid shafts to move up and/or sideways and still turn together. The operation of a worm gear is also shown.

Combining Machines

PRESSES, lathes, milling machines, and boring mills all make parts which are afterward *combined* with each other by bolts and screws to make other useful machines. For example, a typewriter is made up of hundreds of small parts made by many other machines.

Another type of machine combines objects without using bolts or screws, by *welding*. Two edges that are to be welded are brought together; then a ribbon or rod of welding metal is held close to the joint and a white-hot oxyacetylene flame or an electric arc melts it into the joint so that the two edges become one seamless, continuous piece. Among its many other uses, welding is used to join the steel beams of the frames of skyscrapers and the plates of steel ships.

Pieces of metal can also be joined by *riveting*. A hole is drilled into a steel plate and lined up with a hole in another plate. Then a rivet, which looks like a short, heavy steel bolt without threads, is put through the two holes with pincers, and a man called a "bucker" holds a heavy steel bar against the head. Then the "boss" riveter, using a compressed-air riveting gun, flattens the other end of the rivet, joining the two plates tightly together.

Another kind of combining machine is the *automatic loom*, which weaves fabrics from thread or yarn. Crosswise threads, called the *woof*, are interwoven with the lengthwise threads of the *warp* by shuttles which move rapidly back and forth. The result is cloth.

Still another process used to join things together is called *laminating*. Layers of fabric or wood are glued or cemented together by heat and pressure. An automobile tire is built up in this way: layers of fabric, rubber, and cord are formed in molding machines, which, under great heat and pressure, combine the layers permanently.

Plywood panels for building construction are also laminated. A thin ribbon of wood is peeled from around a log, very much as you would peel tape from a roll. This peeling operation is done on a huge lathe with a long, sharp cutting edge. A sheet of this thin wood ribbon is pressed flat, and then another sheet, with the grain at right angles to the first, is glued to it. Other sheets are added, always with the grain reversed, until the panel has the desired thickness. Finally, this wooden "sandwich" is put under a powerful press. The press unites the various layers into one strong sheet, much stronger than a solid wooden plank of the same thickness.

Yet another combining process is the making of synthetic yarns. *Synthetics* are fabrics like nylon, orlon, rayon, and other trade names, whose yarns are made by dissolving wood chips, coal, cotton, and even milk in acids and chemicals to make a substance called *cellulose*

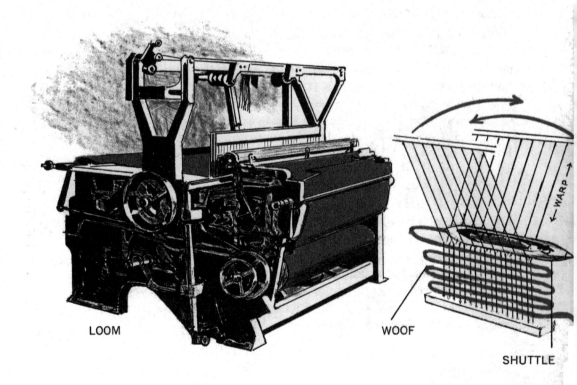

LOOM

WOOF

WARP

SHUTTLE

esters. This is piped into an airtight tank; from there, it is forced out again under pressure through tiny holes in a steel plate called a *spinneret.* This device is named from the tiny gland in a spider's body from which the delicate but strong thread it uses to pin its web.

From the holes in the man-made spinneret, the liquid nylon emerges as many tiny strands, which are joined and twisted into thread or yarn. The yarn goes through an acid bath to toughen it, and is then wound on a spool, or *bobbin*, ready to be woven into fabrics, stockings, and even automobile tires.

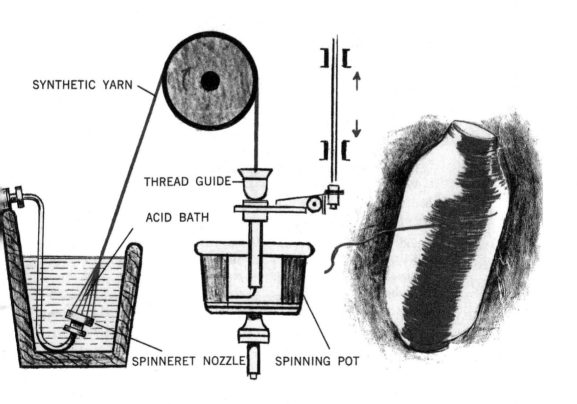

SYNTHETIC YARN

THREAD GUIDE

ACID BATH

SPINNERET NOZZLE   SPINNING POT

Machines That Make the Products We Use Every Day

WE HAVE seen how some machines are designed to make tools and parts used only to build other machines that make the things we need and want. The products of these latter machines can be divided into two main groups. The first group includes such things as shovels, brooms, dishes, beds, blankets, jewelry, bricks, shoes, and all the other millions of products which do their jobs without any mechanical or electrical power in them.

The second group consists of objects which are themselves machines, like automobiles, typewriters, television sets, fans, watches, tractors, and thousands of other. These products all need some kind of mechanical or electrical power to do their jobs.

Of course it takes thousands of different machines to make the millions of products man needs and wants. Some of them are the same machines that make parts for other production machines. Lathes, presses, and planers, for example, are capable of turning out parts for airplanes, trucks, clocks, or percolators. But other machines are especially designed to do one specific job.

Let us take a look at several of these special machines.

When Thomas Edison invented the incandescent lamp, he first had to have his bulbs hand-blown by glass blowers, who could only turn out about 200 bulbs a day.

Today we have the automatic bulb-blowing machine which is so fast that it can turn out a half-million bulbs in one shift. A ribbon of glass flows continuously from the furnace tank onto a flat disc-like wheel with small holes at intervals around its rim. Above each hole is a tube ending in a compressed-air valve. As the glass flows over the hole, a puff of air forces some of the molten glass through the hole, forming a small glass bubble below. Underneath, another wheel at right angles, with molds set around its rim, meets the bubbles and encloses each one within the mold for a moment, while another air blast forces the bubble into the shape of the mold. As the wheel turns, the mold opens, a blast of cold air hardens the bubble—now shaped like a lamp bulb—and automatic shears cut it off neatly and drop it onto a rubber moving belt below. From there it is carried away to be finished·

Another amazing modern machine is the plate-glass machine. Until about fifty years ago all window glass was made by first blowing a glass bubble, lengthening it into a cylinder 40 feet long, and then splitting the cylinder. Then the cylinder was reheated until the glass softened and sagged into a more or less flat sheet. This was slow and costly, and limited the size of the panes.

The modern plate-glass machine begins production with a tank of molten glass, which is kept constantly full. A gob of the molten glass is drawn over a lip of the tank and guided between two rollers which flatten it into a sheet of the right thickness. The sheet keeps drawing more glass from the tank so that there is a continuous ribbon of glass flowing from the tank. This long ribbon is pulled along a series of rollers, gradually cooling until it becomes hard. Then it passes between two huge grinders, which grind it down to remove roughness or distortion.

The ribbon of glass is then cut into 15-foot sheets, which are laid on a moving line of cast-iron tables that pass under huge rotary polishing blocks. With the aid of chemical solutions, the blocks polish the plate glass to gleaming perfection. Then a conveyor line carries the sheets to cutting machines which cut them into different sizes, ready for shipping.

The ribbon of glass from one of these plate-glass machines runs day and night for months, turning out miles of perfect and relatively cheap glass for our modern buildings and automobiles.

Products such as wire, metal rods, pipe, glass tubing, and rods are made by *drawing*. The operation begins at a furnace tank which holds the molten material. At one end of the tank is a nozzle-like device called a *mandrel*, with a hole in it the size of the diameter of wire or tubing desired. The molten material is forced through the hole in the mandrel; as it cools slightly, it is gripped by a kind of pincer and drawn out in a continuous "thread." As the wire cools, it can be wound on big spools. Glass rods run over rollers which keep them straight until they harden, after which they can be cut into desired lengths.

Early automobiles were painted by hand with brushes; then the bodies were hand-rubbed, and given more coats of paint and more rubbing, until the bodies achieved a glossy finish. But later, when cars started coming off assembly lines by the thousands, this method was too slow and costly.

Then the paint sprayer was invented. A car body now enters a long metal tunnel on an endless moving chain where compressed-air nozzles spray on a smooth coat of enamel. The body then travels slowly through the tunnel, where the enamel is baked on at oven heat. When the body emerges from the other end of the tunnel, it has a glittering finish which will last many times longer than the old-fashioned paint-brush job.

To show the broad variety of modern machines today, let us look at a very different type of machine. This is the high-speed facsimile machine used by the telephone and telegraph companies. For many years all that could be sent over wires were the dots and dashes of the telegraph code. Later, Alexander Graham Bell was able to send the human voice over the telephone.

28

But today, with the facsimile machine, one can send letters, orders, payrolls, diagrams, and even drawings by wire. The copy to be sent is simply put on a big drum at one side of the machine. As the drum revolves, it sends thousands of electric impulses out over the wire. These are fed into another facsimile machine in a city perhaps a hundred miles away, where they are changed back into type or lines, reproducing exactly the copy that was sent out.

Machines That Are Themselves Products

THE MACHINES that are themselves products are distinguished by the fact that some kind of mechanical or electric power is always required to run such devices. Of course it would take a long shelf of books to describe the many thousands of machines men use to do the world's work and to make life pleasanter. Nevertheless, we can divide the most important ones into five groups, and examine them one by one:

1. HEAVY MACHINERY. Machines used in road building, excavation and construction, mining, and lumbering.

2. TRANSPORTATION MACHINES. Railroads, planes, ships, automobiles, and trucks.

3. FARMING MACHIINES. Machines used in raising crops.

4. HOUSEHOLD MACHINES. Machines used in the home to prepare food, clean house, and do laundry.

5. OFFICE MACHINES. Machines to keep records, do accounting, write letters, and send out bills.

Heavy Machinery

Among the most important of heavy machinery is that used

in road building. The first roads were simply rough tracks through the wilderness, winding around rocks and swamps and trees. As the country grew more settled, people filled in holes and grubbed out rocks. At first road builders had only picks and shovels and wheelbarrows as tools; later on, wagons pulled by draft animals were used.

The first real road-building machine was probably the horse-drawn scraper, first used in digging the Erie Canal in 1817. Later came harrows to level off the roadbed, followed by heavy rollers pulled by oxen. But when the day of the gasoline engine arrived, there were soon thousands of automobiles and trucks clamoring for someplace to roll. None of the old-fashioned roads, however, were suitable for cars; curves were too sharp, grades too steep, surfaces too rough, and, worst of all, all the roads were too narrow.

In the 1920's, a great wave of road building began—and it has never stopped. The job was so big that new ways of building roads *had* to be found. With the coming of great new superhighways,

ROAD BUILDING MACHINES

more and more power machines were designed to build roads. Let us see how a modern road-building operation works.

As soon as a right of way has been staked out by surveyors, bulldozers and power shovels move in to butt down trees, shove aside great rocks, and scrape dirt into hollows or dump it into huge trucks. After the roadbed has been roughly graded, sheep-foot tampers (big steel rollers with iron bars projecting from them) dig in and loosen the dirt so it can be rolled down evenly.

Next, graders and rollers fill in low places, level bumps, and spread on a layer of gravel and roll it flat. Then steel rails, much like railroad tracks, are laid along each lane to hold the cement in place and allow for expansion. A subgrader, running along these rails, gives the roadbed a final grading. Then comes the gigantic road-layer. At its rear an enormous hopper is lowered, into which cement and sand are dumped from big trucks following behind. Then the hopper pours its load into the mixing drum of the road-layer, and from there through wide-mouthed nozzles

at the other end of the drum, where it is spread evenly between the rails.

Finally a finisher levels off the cement and smoothes the surface. As soon as the cement is dry the new road is ready for traffic.

What kind of heavy machinery is used when a big office building goes up?

Building methods naturally have changed as much over the years as road making has. It is true that ancient tall-spired cathedrals and beautiful palaces were erected without the help of complex machines. And the enormous stones used to build the great pyramids of Egypt were hauled from distant quarries on rollers and lifted in place with inclines and levers as the only tools. But thousands of slaves toiled and died to build the pyramids, and some of the great cathedrals of Europe took over three hundred years to complete.

Modern construction workers have a short working day and good wages. No modern contractor could afford to use labor as freely as in medieval days. Also, no owner could wait years for his building to be finished. Most skyscrapers have to be built in less than two years so that the owners can begin collecting rents to meet their expenses.

Let us see what kinds of heavy machines are needed to put up a building in a hurry. First, a tall crane rumbles alongside the site on its caterpillar treads. A heavy steel ball hanging from a chain at the tip of the crane begins to swing back and forth, slamming against the brick walls of the old houses which must come down so the new building can go up. As soon as the site is cleared, big shovels begin scooping out the hole for the foundation. Next deep holes are drilled and blasted down to bedrock, then filled with cement to serve as bases for the steel columns which will hold up the frame.

32

POWER SHOVEL AND TEN WHEEL TRUCK

The cement arrives in big trucks whose mixing tanks have been constantly revolving on the way from the cement plant. The cement is immediately poured into crane buckets or chutes as soon as the truck arrives.

When the foundations are finished, a big crane starts lifting steel beams into place in the framework. As each one swings into position, the welders or riveters anchor them firmly in place. As the framework rises, extensions are bolted to the crane so it can lift the beams higher.

Next a steel-pipe framework of an elevator shaft rises outside the building frame, with connecting catwalks to each floor. The swift elevator, operated by a donkey engine on the ground, can carry building materials, supplies, and workmen to the floors where they are needed, in a few seconds. Modern bricklayers, or masons, stand on long scaffolds suspended from huge pulleys on wire cables; the scaffolds have wire fences to keep the men from falling off. When one floor is bricked, the scaffold is simply pulled up a few feet to the next floor.

After the outside, or curtain, walls are finished, the floors begin to swarm with plumbers, steam fitters, electricians, plasterers, and other skilled workers who will cover the bare steel and cement skeleton and create apartments or offices. Everywhere one hears electric drills, scrapers, sanders, floor polishers, and many other power tools doing the jobs that men once had to do by hand.

By using all sorts of machines the contractor will have the new building ready for tenants only a few months after the big steel ball began tumbling down the old brick walls.

Heavy machines have also brought about enormous changes in working underground. Mining goes back a good many centuries. The ancient Egyptians were miners; so were the cave dwellers, who dug into the sides of cliffs in search of flints to make their axes and knives.

In later centuries, European miners began to dig deeper mines. They soon found they had to deal with water in the shafts and bad air in the lower tunnels. At first they bailed the water out in buckets pulled up by windlasses; later they used water wheels and windmills to pump it out.

For ventilation the miners simply built fires in the shafts; this heated the foul air and caused it to rise. Fresh cool air would then rush in to take its place.

At first, ore was carried up ladders in baskets. Then windlasses, turned by men or horses, hauled the baskets up by ropes. In the low, cramped *stopes*, or tunnels, the miners had to chip away at the coal or ore with picks, sometimes lying on their backs in pools of water. Their only light was from dim candles or oil lamps mounted on their caps.

Modern mining is a very different story. The shafts and tunnels are brilliantly lighted with electric lamps. Even in the deepest shafts nowadays there is a gentle breeze of fresh air pumped down by great circulators on the surface. Minor flooding is no longer a problem, for big electric pumps keep the tunnels bone-dry.

High-speed elevators take the miners quickly below to the working level. At the working face, or end of the tunnel excavation, the old-time miner had to drill holes into the rock with a hand drill and sledge hammer, fill them with black powder, light a fuse, and run down the tunnel to wait for the explosion. Then he groped his way back through clouds of smoke to break up the fallen chunks of ore with his pick, and shovel them onto a mule-drawn mine car.

Today the machine takes over the whole job. The holes are drilled by compressed-air drills that bore a number of holes at once. The miner rams in smokeless-powder charges in cartridges. From the cartridge caps, wires run back down the tunnel to a magneto box, where the miner presses a plunger to set off the charges.

Next, an automatic loader on caterpillar treads grinds up to the pile of loosened ore, sticks its blunt snout under the pile, and sends the ore on an endless belt to a chute poised over a mine car. In coal mines where there are solid veins of soft coal, a rubber-tire car with a long chain saw reaching out in front of it rolls up to the coal vein. The whirling saw teeth bite into the vein and saw out great blocks of coal.

In some mines, electric rubber-tire trucks take the place of the old car on rails; in others, the ore is dumped onto endless moving rubber belts at the face and delivered to the shaft in a steady stream.

Some mines are called *strip mines* because the ore is near the surface and can be reached by stripping off the layer of earth on top, instead of digging shafts and tunnels. Gigantic power shovels have been built to do the stripping. When the ore is uncovered, it is removed and trucked to the smelter, and the topsoil is replaced so that trees and plants will grow again.

Heavy machinery also plays an important part in lumbering. Before machines were used, trees were felled in winter by loggers using double-bitted axes and handsaws. The logs were then hauled over the snow, on sleds pulled by oxen, to the river bank to await the spring thaw. When spring rains swelled the rivers, the logs were heaved into the water to float downstream to the sawmills, where they were cut into lumber.

Much of the log was wasted in the early mills. Short or crooked limbs, together with bark and sawdust, were simply burned. Only trees growing near large rivers could be lumbered because there

36

was no way to bring logs from the back country to the sawmill.

With the coming of the machine, however, logging railroads were built deep into the forests, opening up new stands of timber far away from rivers. Then, with the "donkey," or stationary engine, a new way of dragging logs to the railroad, without waiting for snow, was discovered. This was called *cable hauling*. A log was made fast to a long steel cable that led through pulleys fastened to trees, and was then snaked cross-country to the rails, by winding the cable around a drum on the donkey engine.

With the arrival of gasoline and Diesel engines, enormous trailer trucks, long enough to carry four or five huge tree trunks, were built. Caterpillar loading cranes lifted the biggest logs onto the trucks. These machines were so powerful they needed no roads. Bulldozers simply knocked out rough trails by butting down trees, shoving aside rocks, and filling deep gullies. Since these logging machines could go almost anywhere in the forest without the expense of building roads, loggers could cut stands of trees never before within reach.

Today, one man with a gasoline-powered chain saw can now cut through a giant tree trunk in less time than it once took ten men with axes and handsaws. Big improvements have come to the sawmills, too. The modern *head rig*, a moving platform with mechanical arms, can pick up a log, turn it over, or move it from side to side. The head sawyer, who controls the head rig from a panel, decides how to cut the log to get the most lumber out of it. Then he moves it toward the whizzing band saw which, cutting through the log like butter, turn it swiftly into boards.

Nowadays, nothing is wasted in a sawmill. Thin sheets of wood are peeled from logs and turned into plywood. Chips and shavings are pressed into sheets called *hardboard*. Other

machines in the pulping mill turn scraps and sawdust into paper, wallboard, plastics, and useful chemicals.

Transportation Machines

Transportation is something which touches all our lives, and the machine plays an ever-increasing role in it.

Trucks carry everything we eat and wear and use. Sleek jet planes now can cross the United States in four hours and the Atlantic in six. Great liners plow the seas at thirty knots. Diesel trains roar over the rails from the Atlantic to the Pacific.

Today most of us take these transportation machines for granted. But let us take a quick look into the past and see what transportation was like before the day of the machine. At first everyone walked and carried his load on his back.

MOTORIZED SAW

Then men began to train animals; soon travelers could ride horses, donkeys, or camels and lead pack animals that carried their baggage.

With the invention of the wheel, it was possible to build carts and wagons, on which much larger loads could be carried. Still, for hundreds of years land transportation was limited by the speed and strength of some draft animal.

Meanwhile, seafarers had known for centuries how to harness the wind. As time passed, shipwrights learned how to build bigger and faster sailing ships. Even so, when there was no wind the nineteenth century clipper-ship captain was no better off than the ancient Egyptian in his Nile barge.

Then, in 1829, an Englishman named George Stephenson thought of mounting one of James Watt's steam engines on a set of wheels. His little locomotive was able to pull a train

of small cars along a track at about twenty miles an hour—
faster than anyone had ever traveled over land before. The
railroad age had dawned.

At about the same time, the American inventor Robert
Fulton mounted a steam engine in a boat and made it turn
a pair of paddle wheels. Steamboats were soon puffing
along all the great rivers, carrying passengers and freight
from town to town. Paddle-wheel ocean steamers always
carried masts and sails in case they ran out of wood; but
presently, screw-propeller vessels, which burned coal,
became reliable, and the sailing ship was doomed.

Just when the steam engine had been so improved that it
seemed it would forever remain the king of transportation,
the gasoline internal-combustion engine was invented.
Instead of getting its power from expanding steam, it worked
by explosions of gasoline vapor. The gas engine opened the
door for the modern automobile, truck, and airplane.

Yet even the gasoline engine was soon to meet stiff competition. The Diesel engine, which burned crude oil instead of more expensive gasoline, was much more efficient. Engineers found that a big Diesel engine could pull a train better and more cheaply than a steam locomotive could. By 1962 only a few scattered steam locomotives were still in service; all the rest had been scrapped and replaced by electric or Diesel engines.

On the highways, too, the Diesel is replacing the gasoline engine in heavy trucks. When you see a big truck with its exhaust pipe sticking straight up in the air behind the cab (instead of underneath), you may be sure it's a Diesel. The reason it is placed there is because its exhaust smoke is too unpleasant to be released near the ground where people are walking.

At sea, the reciprocating engine—whose pistons slide up and down in cylinders to turn the crankshaft—is being rapidly replaced by the turbine engine, which is much more efficient. The turbine works something like a water wheel, except that instead of only a few large blades, the turbine has hundreds of small vanes set in a series of wheels that are tightly enclosed in a casing. Steam at very high pressure is piped into the casing and blown from nozzles against the valves, thus making the turbine wheel revolve.

Still another transportation engine was developed during World War II—the jet engine. Jets work differently from any other engine of the past. Air is sucked into the front intake of the jet engine, mixed with kerosene, and terrifically compressed in a combustion chamber. There it expands under the enormous pressure and roars out of a tube in the rear, forcing the plane ahead.

In some plane engines, the jet, instead of blowing out of a rear tube, is made to drive the blades of a turbine, as steam does in a marine engine The turbine drives the plane's propellers. This is called a *turbo-jet* engine.

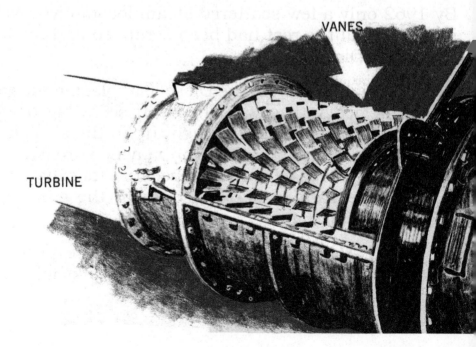

VANES

TURBINE

Farming Machines

One of the most important jobs of modern machines is to help the farmer grow our food. With machines, today's farmer can raise enough food to feed many city people. On our trip through medieval England, we saw how the peasants had to plant, cultivate, and reap their crops with shovels, rakes, sickles, and other hand tools. Four out of five people had to work on the land, because they could raise so little using these crude methods.

The first crude plows were only sharpened tree limbs. Later, plows with wooden or iron plowshares that could plow a deeper furrow were invented. Wood- or steel-toothed harrows replaced the rake and hoe. In more modern times, horse-drawn mowing and reaping machines harvested the hay and grain much faster than the scythe and sickle could.

The great step forward came when farmers began to use steam and gasoline engines. One mechanized farmer could do as much work as ten men with hand tools. Today the mechanical spreader spreads fertilizer over the fields followed by a tractor-drawn gang plow which plows many furrows at one time. Hitched behind the plow, harrows and rollers smooth and roll the field so that the ground is ready for seeding in one operation. Instead of sowing seed by hand, the farmer fills the bin of his *drill*, or seeder, hooks it onto his tractor and drives across the field. The drill digs a number of furrows, drops in the seed automatically, and then covers over the furrows.

During the growing season power cultivators plow under the weeds, and sprayers travel over the rows, spraying the plants to kill insects. Often crops in large fields are "dusted" with insect-killing powder spread from tanks in low-flying planes.

When the crops are ripe, big machines called *combines*,

pulled by tractors, sweep over the great wheat fields, cutting wide swaths of grain with the sharp teeth of their reaper arms. The cut grain is then swept up into the machine on a moving belt where it is threshed. The kernels of grain pour through chutes into bags which are closed automatically when filled and dumped out of the other side of the combine into trucks following alongside. Meanwhile, straw is being pressed into bales, bound with wire, and tossed into other trucks.

Other harvesting machines pick corn, beans, potatoes, tomatoes, and many other crops. Scything and pitching hay by hand are also becoming operations of the past. Hay is now cut and baled by machines; the bales are then lifted into haylofts by motor loaders.

The modern farm has as much machinery in its buildings as a small machine shop. In the cowbarn, electric milking machines can milk a whole row of cows at the same time. Electric separators remove the cream from the milk, and power churns make the butter. Electricity lights the buildings and pumps the water. Power lathes, drills, grinders, and welders help keep the farm machines and

DISC PLOW AND HARROW

tools in repair. Each year machines and scientific farming make it possible for fewer farmers to feed more and more people.

Household Machines

Every moment of the day we can see how the machine has made life easier and pleasanter in our homes.

But what about a home of 150 years ago? Winter meant sawing and chopping cord after cord of firewood, building fires in each fireplace in the morning, and feeding these fires all day. Today, when it gets cool, the thermostat in the hall turns on an oil or gas burner in the basement, and turns if off again when it becomes warm enough.

In that same house of 150 years ago, ice had to be cut in a pond and stored in an icehouse. The chunks had to be carried to an icebox, and the drip pan under it often had to be emptied. Now quiet, work-free refrigerators and deep-freezers do the job.

Once, all meals were cooked in the fireplace in kettles or pots hanging from a crane. Meat was roasted on a spit, kept

COMBINE

turning by a slave child or a dog on a treadmill. Today, gas or electric ranges cook the food to any desired temperature, and the stove will turn itself off at whatever time the dial is set for.

Floors and carpets were once cleaned by scrub brushes and brooms—and plenty of muscle power. Now it can all be done by electricity, with rotary scrubbers, waxers, and vacuum cleaners. Once toast was made on a fork held over the coals, and coffee beans were ground in the kitchen and boiled in a tin pot. Wash day saw mother bent over a steaming tub, rubbing clothes clean on a washboard, then hanging them out to dry on a line. And the flatiron she had to press them with had to be heated over a wood stove.

Now we have electric toasters, percolators, roto-broilers, blenders, fans, steam irons, clock-radios and dishwashers. Electric washing machines, driers, and irons take the back-breaking work out of wash day. For outdoor chores, there are power mowers with attachments to suck up grass cuttings, chop them up, and blow them into a bag. Electric hedge clippers trim the hedges. From the early morning clamor of the electric clock-radio to the switching on of the electric blanket at bedtime, machines make work and play at home pleasanter.

Office Machines

The machine is very much a part of the modern business office. A hundred years ago, if you opened the door of a business office you would have seen a row of clerks wearing eyeshades and sleeve garters, sitting on high stools before tall, slant-top desks. You would have heard the scratching of goose-quill pens entering long columns of figures in massive ledgers. The columns had to be added in the heads of the clerks, who also wrote orders and answered letters in longhand.

There was no carbon paper either, with which to make

copies of letters and other documents. So, all letters, written with purple copying ink, were placed between two pages of a tissue-paper copy book with a damp cloth pad on top to moisten the ink. Then the copy book was placed under a letter press, which squeezed it, leaving a blurred copy of the letter on the tissue page.

Today, a modern business office must handle mountains of records, letters, bills, statements, and other data, all of which must be checked, answered, and filed. Without office machines this mass of paper work could never be kept up with.

The first machine to revolutionize office work was the typewriter, introduced about the year 1874. Its success spurred inventors to develop machines that added, divided, and multiplied columns of figures quickly and correctly. Also, it took too long to hunt for information in dog-eared ledgers and cardboard letter files, so machines were invented to speed this up. They contained thousands of punched cards, each with specific information. If a company wanted to know which of its customers had bought a certain model of its machine, the operator pressed several buttons, and cards with the names of all those customers came out of a slot.

Special typewriters now can type information on a tape, which is fed into a card-punch machine where that same information is punched out on the cards. The tape may even be put into a telephone sender, flashed over long-distance wires, and fed into a card-punch machine hundreds of miles away.

Automation, and Machines That "Think"

THE NEWEST, and perhaps most exciting, machines today are the electric computers. Problems that would take a team of men years to figure out are fed into the computer. Gears turn, transistors and tubes light up, and in a few minutes out comes the correct answer! Machine designers are now building machines with so-called electric "brains," which appear to "think" for themselves.

This new idea in machines is called *automation*—its aim is to take over the dull, monotonous jobs which require little skill in factories. While the machines do these jobs, more men will be freed to inspect work, sharpen tools, keep the machines running, and attend to other important jobs.

Let us see how one of these machines is made to "think" for itself. Alongside the machine is a console containing a panel of control buttons, and a roll of tape on which is typed the symbols that will direct the machine.

Engineers have been specially trained to turn the instructions they want to give the machine into these symbols. The tape unrolls and passes before a *scanner*, which turns the symbols into electric impulses. These go over a maze of wires into a tall steel cabinet filled with the switching gear of the computer. The circuits lead to small electric motors in the machine itself, which are turned on or off by the electrical impulses. In this way, a computer can be made to perform many tasks.

Here is an example of how automation works. A chassis of an automatic scale needs holes drilled into it in different places and at different angles. Before automation, a man would have had to bolt the drilling mechanism into one machine, set the proper tool, bore the hole, and then remove it. Then he would have to bolt it into another machine to do another operation and so on until the work was finished.

With automation, an impulse goes to the electronic "brain" which tells the machine to pick up tool #4 from a big wheel which holds various tools in slots around its rim.

48

The wheel turns until #4 slot is opposite an arm, which picks out the tool and clamps it into place. Then another impulse tells the machine to start boring. When the hole is deep enough, the "brain" stops the drill, returns it to its slot, and waits for another order. In this way, the tape continues to flow along, step by step, telling the machine what to do, until the work on the chassis is finished and it slides along a belt to make room for the next part.

Scientists tell us that we are on the brink of even greater discoveries in electronics and machine design. Who knows what machines will be able to do before the year 2000? Most of you will be here to find out—you are living in an exciting time.

AUTOMATION: TAPE CONTROLLED MACHINE

Index

CPSIA information can be obtained
at www.ICGtesting.com
Printed in the USA
BVOW07s1917021117
499386BV00004B/72/P